Residential Energy Tax Credits: Overview and Analysis

Margot L. Crandall-Hollick
Analyst in Public Finance

Molly F. Sherlock
Specialist in Public Finance

September 25, 2012

Congressional Research Service

7-5700

www.crs.gov

R42089

CRS Report for Congress ————————————————
Prepared for Members and Committees of Congress

Summary

Currently, taxpayers may be able to claim two tax credits for residential energy efficiency: one is scheduled to expire at the end of 2011, whereas the other is scheduled to expire at the end of 2016. The nonbusiness energy property tax credit (Internal Revenue Code (IRC) §25C) currently provides homeowners with a tax credit for investments in certain high-efficiency heating, cooling, and water-heating appliances, as well as tax credits for energy-efficient windows and doors. For installations made during 2011, the credit rate was 10%, with a maximum credit amount of $500. The credit available during 2011 was less than what had been available during 2009 and 2010, when taxpayers were allowed a 30% tax credit of up to $1,500 for making energy-efficiency improvements to their homes. The residential energy efficient property credit (IRC §25D), which provides a 30% tax credit for investments in properties that generate renewable energy, such as solar panels, is scheduled to remain available through 2016.

Advances in energy efficiency have allowed per-capita residential energy use to remain relatively constant since the 1970s, even as demand for energy-using technologies has increased. Experts believe, however, that there is unrealized potential for further residential energy efficiency. One reason investment in these technologies might not be at optimal levels is that certain market failures result in energy prices that are too low. If energy is relatively inexpensive, consumers will not have a strong incentive to purchase a technology that will lower their energy costs. Tax credits are one policy option to potentially encourage consumers to invest in energy-efficiency technologies.

Residential energy-efficiency tax credits were first introduced in the late 1970s, but were allowed to expire in 1985. Tax credits for residential energy efficiency were again enacted as part of the Energy Policy Act of 2005 (P.L. 109-58). These credits were expanded and extended as part of the American Recovery and Reinvestment Act of 2009 (ARRA; P.L. 111-5). The Section 25C credit was again extended, at a reduced rate, and with a reduced cap, through 2011, as part of the Tax Relief, Unemployment Insurance Reauthorization, and Job Creation Act of 2010 (P.L. 111-312).

Although the purpose of residential energy-efficiency tax credits is to motivate additional energy-efficiency investment, the amount of the investment resulting from these credits is unclear. Purchasers investing in energy-efficient property for other reasons—for example concern about the environment—would have invested in such property absent tax incentives, and hence stand to receive a windfall gain from the tax benefit. Further, the fact that the incentive is delivered as a nonrefundable credit limits the provision's ability to motivate investment for low- and middle-income taxpayers with limited tax liability. The administration of residential energy-efficiency tax credits has also had compliance issues, as identified in a recent Treasury Department Inspector General for Tax Administration (TIGTA) report.

There are various policy options available for Congress to consider regarding incentives for residential energy efficiency. One option is to let the existing tax incentives expire as scheduled. A second option would be to extend or modify the current tax incentives. S. 3521, the Family and Business Tax Cut Certainty Act of 2012, would extend the 25C credit for two years—2012 and 2013. Another option would be to replace the current tax credits with a grant or rebate program—the Home Star Energy Retrofit Act of 2010 (H.R. 5019 / S. 3177 in the 111th Congress), for example. Grants or rebates could be made more widely available, and not be limited to taxpayers with tax liability. Enacting a grant or rebate program, however, would have additional budgetary cost.

Contents

Figures

Tables

Appendixes

Contacts

Introduction

Residential energy efficiency can benefit consumers through reduced utility bills, and support national environmental policy objectives by reducing the demand for electricity generated using fossil-fuels and reducing current strains on the electric power grid. Various policies to increase conservation and energy efficiency have been adopted since the 1970s, including tax incentives.[1] Developing and deploying technologies that are consistent with the most efficient use of our nation's energy resources is broadly appealing. What remains unclear, however, is what set of policy tools the federal government should employ to meet energy-efficiency objectives.

In 2010, 23% of total energy consumed in the United States was consumed by the residential sector (see **Figure 1**). Residential-sector energy use has been increasing over time, with the residential sector today consuming roughly 8% more energy in 2010 than in 2000. Residential energy use per capita, however, has remained relatively constant since the 1970s (see **Figure 2**). Thus, while overall demand for energy in the residential sector has increased with population growth, efficiency gains have allowed residential energy use per capita to remain relatively flat even as consumers increasingly use energy-demanding technologies.

Figure 1. U.S. Energy Consumption by Sector

2010

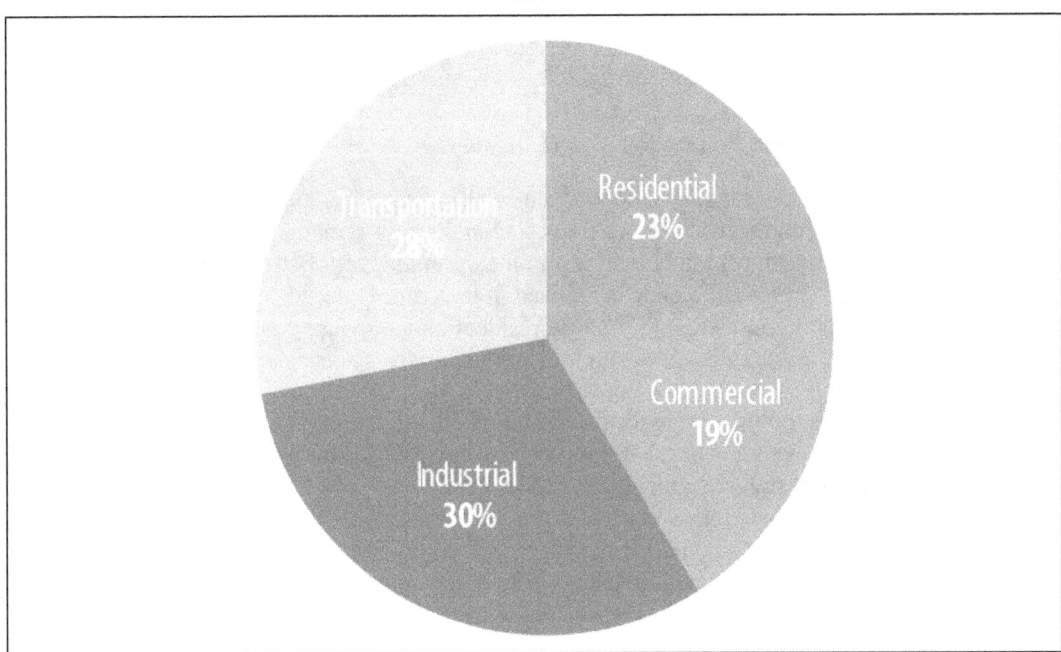

Source: U.S. Energy Information Administration, Annual Energy Review, October 19, 2011.
Notes: Total energy consumption in each end-use sector includes primary energy consumption, electricity retail sales, and electrical system energy losses.

---

[1] Policies that have been adopted to support energy efficiency and conservation, that are beyond the scope of this report, include research and development (R&D) funding, pilot programs, and efficiency standards and mandates.

Figure 2. Residential Energy Use Trends

1949 - 2010

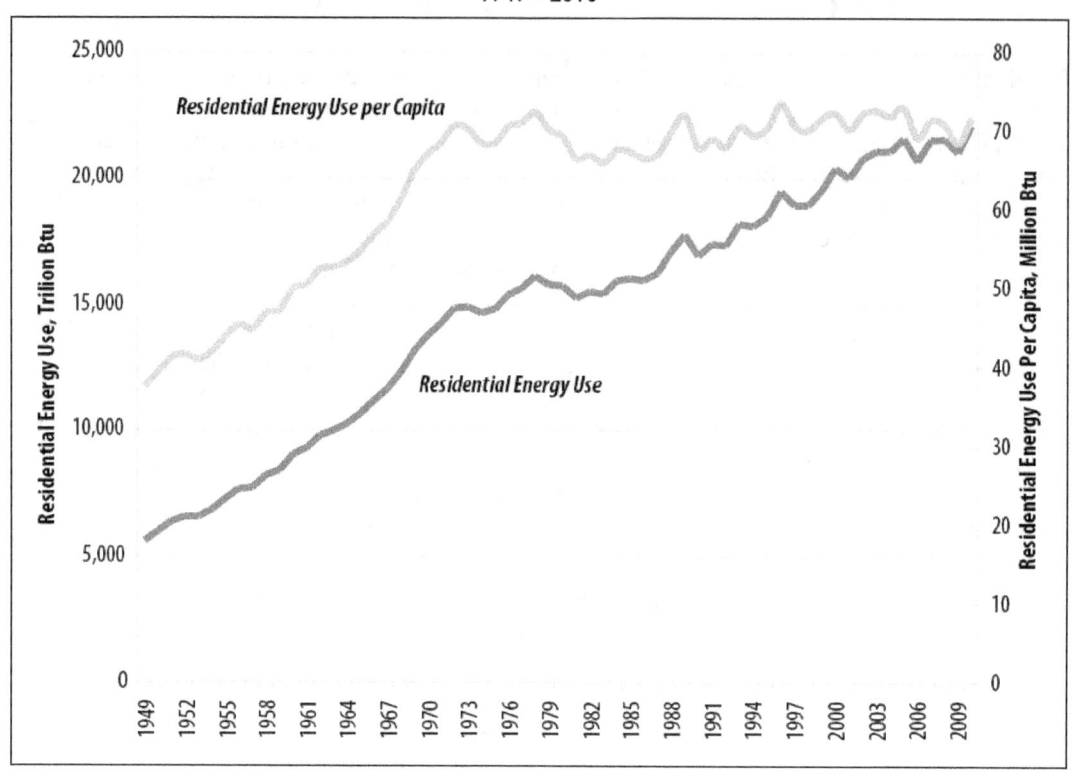

Source: Energy Information Administration, Annual Energy Review, October 19, 2011.

Although energy-efficiency gains have been made in recent decades, experts suggest that a large potential for increased energy efficiency in the residential sector remains.[2] Despite this potential, concerns remain that consumers may not invest in the optimal level of energy efficiency. If this potential for enhanced energy efficiency is realized in the coming decades, residential energy use trends could change, perhaps leading to reduced residential energy use per capita over time. However, population growth may still result in continued increases in total residential energy use.

This report explores one policy option for promoting residential energy efficiency: tax credits. It begins by providing an overview of the current residential energy-efficiency tax credits[3] (appendices to this report provide a more detailed legislative history). The report then goes on to provide an economic rationale for residential energy-efficiency tax incentives, introducing the concept of "market failures" and "market barriers" which may lead to suboptimal or "economically inefficient" investment in energy-efficiency technologies. That section summarizes various market failures and market barriers in the residential energy sector and outlines ways tax incentives correct them. The final sections of this report provide an economic

---

[2] For example, see Hannah Choi Granade, John Creyts, and Anton Derkach, et al., *Unlocking Energy Efficiency in the U.S. Economy*, McKinsey & Company, July 2009, http://www.mckinsey.com/Client_Service/ Electric_Power_and_Natural_Gas/Latest_thinking/Unlocking_energy_efficiency_in_the_US_economy.aspx.

[3]The terms "residential energy-efficiency credits" and "residential energy credits" are used interchangeably in this report. The Internal Revenue Services refers to these credits as "residential energy credits."

---

analysis of the primary tax incentives for residential energy efficiency and briefly review various policy options.

Current Law

In 2011, taxpayers are eligible to claim tax credits for expenditures related to residential energy-efficiency and residential renewable-energy generation technologies. The first credit, the nonbusiness energy property tax credit (IRC §25C), allows taxpayers to claim a tax credit for energy-efficiency improvements they make to the building envelope (insulation, windows, doors) of their primary residence and for the purchase of high-efficiency heating, cooling, and water-heating appliances they purchase for their primary residence.[4] The amount of the credit is calculated as 10% of expenditures on building envelope improvements plus the cost of each energy-efficient property capped at a specific amount (ranging from $50 to $300), excluding labor and installation costs. Given the price of high-efficiency heating, cooling, and water-heating appliances, taxpayers generally claim the maximum amount of the credit for energy-efficient property. The maximum value of the credit is capped at $500. This cap applies to claims for the Section 25C credit made in the current year, as well as those made in the prior tax year. In other words, if a taxpayer claimed $500 or more of the Section 25C credit prior to 2011, they cannot claim it in 2011. **Table 1** summarizes eligibility requirements for residential energy-efficiency tax credits in 2011.

Table 1. Residential Energy-Efficiency Tax Credits in 2011

	Section 25C Credit	Section 25D Credit
Calculation of credit	10% of Qualifying Energy-Efficiency Improvements + Qualifying Energy Property	30% of Energy Efficient Property
Types of Qualifying Property	**Qualifying Energy-efficiency Improvements** (1) Insulation (2) Windows (Including Skylights) (3) Doors (4) Qualifying Metal Roof (5) Asphalt Roof with Cooling Granules **Energy Property and Associated Caps** (1) Electric Heat Pump; Central Air Conditioner; Natural Gas, Propane, or Oil Water Heater; Biomass Stove: $300 (3) Natural Gas, Propane or Oil Furnace or Hot Water Boiler: $150 (4) Advanced Main Air Circulating Fan: $50	**Energy Efficient Property** (1) Solar Electric (2) Solar Water Heating (3) Fuel Cell: $500 per 0.5kW of Capacity (4) Small Wind Energy (5) Geothermal Heat Pumps
Credit Cap	$200 for windows (lifetime cap) $500 (lifetime cap)	None
Scheduled Expiration	December 31, 2011	December 31, 2016

Source: CRS analysis of P.L. 109-58, P.L. 109-432, P.L. 110-343, P.L. 111-5, and P.L. 111-312.

---

[4] This residence must be an existing home, not a new home.

The second credit, the residential energy efficient property tax credit (IRC §25D), allows taxpayers to claim a tax credit for properties that generate renewable energy (e.g., solar panels, geothermal heat pumps, small wind energy, fuel cells) that they install on their residence.[5] The amount of the credit is calculated as 30% of expenditures on technologies that generate renewable energy, including labor and installation costs. The maximum value of the Section 25D credit for renewable-energy-generating technologies other than fuel cells is not capped.[6] The Section 25C credit is scheduled to expire at the end of 2011, whereas the Section 25D credit is scheduled to expire at the end of 2016.[7] S. 3521, the Family and Business Tax Cut Certainty Act of 2012, would extend the Section 25C credit for two years—2012 and 2013. For more detailed information on the Section 25C and Section 25D credits, including eligible energy-efficiency property specifications, see **Appendix A**. A comprehensive legislative history of these credits can be found in **Appendix B**.

The Economic Rationale for Residential Energy-Efficiency Tax Credits

A rational consumer would be expected to invest in an energy-efficiency technology if the savings that resulted from using the property were greater than the cost of the property. For example, if insulation was expected to lower home-heating costs to such an extent that the homeowner fully recovered the costs of the insulation through lower heating bills, the homeowner would be expected to make this purchase. However, some consumers appear to forgo making these investments, which is known as the "energy-efficiency paradox."

Various economic theories may help explain why consumers do not invest in the optimal amount of residential energy efficiency. Certain "market failures" related to both the production and consumption of energy may help explain why consumers do not make more investments in energy-efficiency technologies, such that the optimal or "economically efficient" number of consumers use these technologies. In addition to these market failures, other market barriers to investment in residential energy efficiency have been identified.[8] The Section 25C and Section 25D credits do not directly correct for some of the market failures and market barriers discussed below, which may limit their impact on increasing energy efficiency.

---

[5] For all technologies, except fuel cells, the credit can be claimed for installations of renewable-energy-generating technologies made to any of the taxpayers' residences, not just a principal residence. Eligible fuel cell installation must be made on a taxpayer's primary residence.

[6] The credit for fuel cells is called at $500 per 0.5W of power capacity.

[7] The renewable-energy-generating technology must be placed in service before December 31, 2016.

[8] As part of the Energy Policy Act of 2005 (P.L. 109-58), Congress established an advisory committee to study this issue. In 2007, the advisory committee released a report, *Carbon Lock-In: Barriers to Deploying Climate Change Mitigation Technologies.* An analysis of this report can be found in CRS Report R40670, *Energy Efficiency in Buildings: Critical Barriers and Congressional Policy*, by Paul W. Parfomak, Fred Sissine, and Eric A. Fischer. This report presents market barriers likely to prevent efficient adoption of energy-efficient technologies, drawing on both the *Carbon Lock-In* report and the economics literature on energy-efficient technology adoption.

Market Failures and Market Barriers

There are a variety of reasons why consumers may not make optimal investments in residential energy efficiency. Market failures, including both externalities and principal-agent problems, provide one possible explanation. Other market barriers, including capital market imperfections and informational issues, may also help explain suboptimal investment in residential energy efficiency.

Energy consumption externalities are a potential reason why markets may underallocate resources for residential energy-efficiency investment. Broadly, an externality is a cost or benefit associated with a transaction that is not reflected in market prices. Specifically, residential electricity consumption may be associated with negative environmental externalities, such as pollution costs. If electricity prices do not reflect any potential negative environmental consequences of electricity production, consumers do not pay the full cost associated with consuming electricity. These lower prices lead consumers to consume more electricity than is optimal, and to underinvest in energy efficiency.[9]

Conversely, the adoption of newly developed energy-efficient technologies may result in positive externalities via "knowledge spillover" effects. For example, if one homeowner pays for and installs a new type of solar panel on his home, his neighbors may see this technology, learn about it, and be more likely to adopt it themselves.[10] These knowledge spillover effects mean that, in addition to the benefits to each individual consumer, the adoption of emerging technologies has a greater benefit to society as a whole. Since markets fail to consider the benefits associated with knowledge spillover effects, more of the technology should be adopted than is adopted under the market forces of supply and demand.[11]

Another type of market failure, the principal-agent problem, can occur when there is a disconnect between the incentives for those making energy-efficient property purchasing decisions (the agent) and the ultimate energy consumer (the principal). For example, in non-owner-occupied housing, landlords (agents) may underinvest in energy efficiency when tenants (principals) pay the utility bills.[12] Builders of new homes may also install lower-cost, less efficient technologies if they do not believe the cost of installing high-efficiency products can be recovered when the property is sold. Since the landlord and the builder make decisions regarding the level of energy-efficiency investment, without knowing the energy use patterns of the end user (the tenant or homebuyer), landlords and builders may not invest in the optimal amount of energy efficiency.

---

[9] As an example, consider an individual running an energy-using appliance, such as an air conditioner. While the individual may consider the impact of the air conditioner on their electricity bill, they are unlikely to think about the CO_2 emissions associated with generating the electricity necessary to power the air conditioner. If carbon emissions are not priced, and parties involved in transactions involving carbon emissions do not pay for the environmental cost of such emissions, the market outcome will result in a higher level of emissions than is socially optimal.

[10] Knowledge spillover benefits are most likely to result when consumers are considering adoption of new technologies. Many of the products currently eligible for energy-efficiency tax incentives incorporate technologies that have been available for a number of years, and are thus not new to the market.

[11] Adam B. Jaffe, Richard G. Newell, and Robert N. Stavins, "Technology Policy for Energy and the Environment," in *Innovation Policy and the Economy*, ed. Adam B. Jaffe, Josh Lerner, and Scott Stern, 4th ed. (Cambridge, MA: The MIT Press, 2004), pp. 35-68.

[12] This assumes that landlords are not able to capture the benefits of greater energy efficiency through higher rents.

Capital market imperfections may also lead households to underinvest in energy-efficiency property. Oftentimes, investments in energy efficiency involve high initial costs, followed by a flow of savings. Purchasers unable to obtain funds up front may purchase less expensive, less efficient alternatives. Low-income households tend to be more credit constrained, and therefore more likely to settle for less energy-efficient alternatives when unable to borrow cash up front.[13]

Finally, when consumers lack information about energy-saving technologies, they may be unaware of the opportunity to make such investments. If consumers have some, but not all the information relevant to make investments in energy-efficiency technologies, they may still be less willing to make these purchases. For example, uncertainty about future energy prices may make consumers reluctant to make irreversible energy-property investments.

How Tax Credits May Address Market Failures and Market Barriers

Various government policies can be used to enhance the functioning of markets in the face of market failures or market barriers. Tax incentives are one option. Other policy options, which are beyond the scope of this report, might include non-tax incentives, such as grants, rebates, or credit enhancements. (Although one particular grant program, Energy Star, is briefly discussed as a policy option at the end of this report, a comprehensive analysis of this policy option is not provided in this report.) The government may also choose to address energy market failures using regulations or mandates. Governments can also support investments in energy efficiency through informational programs (e.g., the Energy Star labeling program).

Policymakers can attempt to correct negative externalities associated with residential energy consumption by using tax credits like the Section 25C and Section 25D credits to lower the cost of energy-efficiency investments, thereby motivating additional investment in these technologies. Other tax incentives not discussed in this report, like the energy-efficient appliance manufacturer credit (IRC §45M), which lowers the cost of producing energy-efficient appliances (known as a "supply-side" incentive), may also bring down the cost of certain technologies. (For a list of residential energy-efficiency tax incentives, see **Appendix C**, **Table C-1**.) By encouraging additional investment, the availability of tax credits may also address the positive externalities that result from energy-efficiency technologies in terms of increased awareness about these technologies. Governments can also increase knowledge about technologies with information programs like the Energy Star labeling program.

However, if markets underinvest in energy efficiency because electricity prices are artificially low, tax credits are not the most economically efficient policy option for increasing energy-efficiency investment. Tax credits result in federal revenue losses and can provide windfall gains to taxpayers. The most efficient way to increase investment in energy efficiency under these circumstances would be to allow electricity prices to fully reflect electricity costs. This could be done by removing existing federal financial support for electricity (e.g., energy-related tax subsidies) or by taxing electricity production that generates external costs not currently reflected in market prices. Increasing the price of electricity such that consumers face the full costs

---

[13] Low income borrowers that are given loans are likely to face higher interest rates. Since low income individuals face higher interest rates, they are likely to use a higher discount rate when evaluating energy-saving investments. When evaluated using a higher discount rate, fewer projects will appear to have long-run cost savings.

associated with electricity consumption would encourage increased investment in energy-efficiency technologies.

Most currently available tax incentives for residential energy efficiency do not directly address the principal-agent problem discussed earlier. The Section 25C and Section 25D credits are not available to renters, and thus do not directly encourage renters to invest in residential energy efficiency. Further, since the Section 25C and Section 25D credits cannot be claimed for investments made to rental property, landlords do not benefit from incentives designed to encourage residential energy-efficiency investments. Other tax incentives not discussed in this report, like the tax credit for energy-efficient new homes (IRC §45L), more directly address potential principal-agent problems in the market for new homes.

Tax credits, which may be claimed several months after eligible purchases are made, will have limited effect in overcoming capital market imperfections for homeowners who may be unable to secure credit to pay for the upfront costs associated with energy-efficient technologies. Although tax incentives for residential energy efficiency do reduce the cost of investment, tax credits may not be the most effective policy option for providing immediate savings to consumers that are credit constrained.[14]

Although the two tax credits analyzed in this report are designed to encourage additional investment in residential energy-efficient property in existing homes, they may not rectify other existing market failures, limiting their ability to increase usage of energy-efficient technologies to their optimal or economically efficient levels.

Analysis of Residential Energy Tax Credits

The following sections provide a brief economic analysis of the Section 25C and Section 25D tax credits, evaluating their behavioral effects on increasing investment, their fairness or equity, and potential administrative issues. From an economic standpoint, tax incentives are effective if they succeed in causing taxpayers to engage in the desired behavior. In the case of residential energy-efficiency tax benefits, it is not clear how effective such tax credits are at causing additional investment, as opposed to rewarding consumers that would have made investments absent tax incentives. Residential energy tax credits also tend to benefit higher-income taxpayers, an issue which is explored in detail below. Finally, the Treasury Inspector General for Tax Administration (TIGTA) has identified administrative issues with the current tax benefits for residential energy efficiency. The results of their report are also summarized below.

Efficiency: Do Tax Credits Motivate Residential Energy-Efficiency Investments?

The goal of residential energy-efficiency tax credits is to encourage individuals to increase residential energy-efficiency investments. From the government's perspective, these tax policies

---

[14] As an alternative, grants or rebates that reduce the cost of energy-efficient property at the time of purchase, are a more direct mechanism for reducing up front costs. If capital market imperfections are preventing investment in energy-efficient technologies, a consumer loan program would be a more direct option for addressing this market barrier.

are successful if tax credits cause additional residential energy-efficiency investment. If, however, tax credits simply reward consumers for investments that would have been made absent such tax incentives, then the tax incentives are not achieving the policy goal. Tax credits that reward consumers for residential energy-efficiency investments, rather than lead consumers to make additional residential energy-efficiency investments, provide a windfall gain to credit recipients without resulting in additional economy-wide energy-efficiency investment or reduced energy consumption.

Concerns that tax credits for residential energy efficiency may not generate additional investment were raised when such credits were first introduced in the 1970s. In 1979, one year after residential energy tax credits were first introduced, several Members of Congress voiced their reservations about these tax credits in a series of House Ways and Means hearings on President Carter's proposals to expand residential energy tax benefits. During one of these hearings, Representative Bill Frenzel remarked,

> I am nervous about tax credits. The principal tax credit bill we passed last year does not seem to have given great incentive in the marketplace. The drain on Treasury has been less than we expected because people did not flock to take advantage of it. The tax credit tends to be a reward for economic action that was forced by other factors. The tax credit does not motivate, but rather simply occurs at the end of the year when the fellow finds out there was a tax credit available. And I do not think that is a very efficient and effective stimulus.[15]

Empirical evidence evaluating whether the residential energy tax credits available in the late 1970s and early 1980s caused additional investment in energy-efficiency property is mixed. Although some researchers found that tax incentives that reduced the price of energy-efficiency property would lead to additional investment,[16] others found that the tax credits were instead more likely associated with windfall gains to credit recipients as opposed to additional energy-efficiency investment.[17] Whether tax credits can result in additional energy-efficiency investment remains an issue to be considered by policymakers evaluating options for encouraging enhanced residential energy-efficiency investment.

There are several reasons why residential energy tax credits may not have a significant impact on purchasing decisions for many consumers. First, consumers investing in residential energy-efficiency improvements may be responding to other market incentives, such as the high price of energy. For the consumer that would have invested in residential energy-efficiency property without the tax incentive, federal revenue losses associated with the tax credit are windfall gains to the consumer. Second, savings associated with tax credits are not realized until tax returns are filed, often months after energy-efficiency property is purchased. This reduces the incentive power of the credit. Third, tax credits only reduce the price of investment in residential energy-efficiency property for taxpayers having income tax liability to offset with credits. Estimates suggest that in 2011, 46% of U.S. households will have no federal income tax liability, meaning

---

[15] U.S. Congress, House Committee on Ways and Means, *The President's Energy Program, Phase III*, committee print, 96th Cong., 1st sess., July 1979, p. 317.

[16] See Kevin A. Hassett and Gilbert E. Metcalf, "Energy Tax Credits and Residential Conservation Investment: Evidence from Panel Data," *Journal of Public Economics*, vol. 57, no. 2 (June 1995), pp. 201-217.

[17] See Michael J. Walsh, "Energy Tax Credits and Housing Improvement," *Energy Economics*, vol. 11, no. 4 (October 1989), pp. 275-284 and Jeffery A. Dubin and Steven E. Henson, "The Distributional Effects of the Federal Energy Tax Act," *Resources and Energy*, vol. 10, no. 3 (1988), pp. 191-212.

that tax credits for energy-efficiency investment do not provide a current financial incentive for such investments for these taxpayers.[18]

Tax incentives for residential energy efficiency are most likely to motivate energy-efficiency investments for certain types of taxpayers. As noted above, tax incentives only create a financial incentive for investment for taxpayers with tax liability. Thus, higher-income taxpayers are more likely to benefit from residential energy-efficiency tax incentives. Higher-income taxpayers are also more likely to be motivated to invest in residential energy efficiency through tax incentives. Tax credits may also motivate those already in the market for energy property to make more efficient choices. If consumers choose to invest in certain residential energy-efficiency equipment, such as heating and cooling property, only when existing units are no longer operational, tax credits might motivate the purchase of high-efficiency units amongst taxpayers with tax liability.

Equity: Who Benefits from Residential Energy Tax Credits?

The purpose of residential energy-efficiency tax incentives is to increase investment in energy efficiency and properties that generate renewable energy. For these tax credits to be effective, they must be targeted at individuals and households that make choices regarding energy property investments. For residential credits, the target population is homeowners. Taxpayers that are homeowners tend to be higher income than taxpayers living in renter-occupied housing.[19] Hence, it would be expected that energy tax incentives targeted at homeowners would tend to benefit higher-income taxpayers.

This is borne out in tax data, as residential energy-efficiency tax credits are predominantly claimed by middle-and upper-income taxpayers (see **Table 2** and **Figure 3**). In 2009, roughly three-quarters (75.7%) of residential energy tax credits claims were made on tax returns with adjusted gross income (AGI) above $50,000.[20] In addition, these tax units claimed 82.5% of the total value of residential credits in 2009. Although tax units with incomes below $50,000 compose two-thirds (66.1%) of all tax units, less than one quarter (24.4%) of tax units in this income class claim residential energy tax credits, claiming less than 18% of the total value of these credits. In addition, as a tax unit's income rises, the average amount of its residential credit also rises, such that tax units with the highest income level receive on average a credit that is more than eight times the average credit value for the lowest income tax unit.

---

[18] See Rachel Johnson, James Nunns, and Jeffrey Rohaly, et al., *Why Some Tax Units Pay No Income Tax*, Tax Policy Center: Urban Institute: Brookings Institution, July 2011, http://www.taxpolicycenter.org/UploadedPDF/1001547-Why-No-Income-Tax.pdf; and CRS Report R41362, *Who Doesn't Pay Income Taxes?*, by Thomas L. Hungerford.

[19] According to the American Housing Survey, in 2009 the median income of homeowners was $60,000 compared to $28,400 for renters.[19]

[20] In this section, tax returns and tax units are used interchangeably and include returns with no taxable income. A tax unit is not necessarily an individual, but represents all the individuals included on an income tax return including spouses and dependents.

**Table 2. Distribution and Average Amount of Residential Energy Tax Credits, by
Adjusted Gross Income, 2009**

Adjusted Gross Income	Percentage of All Tax Returns	Percentage of Tax Returns Claiming Residential Credits	Percentage of Total Amount of Credit (Revenue Loss)	Average Amount of Credit
$0-$15K	26.8%	0.9%	0.2%	$171.61
$15K-$30K	21.4%	6.6%	3.8%	$502.58
$30K-$50K	17.9%	16.9%	13.5%	$692.32
$50K-$75K	13.3%	23.3%	21.7%	$810.60
$75K-$100K	8.2%	19.1%	18.8%	$857.10
$100K-$200K	9.6%	26.6%	30.4%	$994.22
$200K and above	2.8%	6.7%	11.5%	$1,486.06
TOTAL	100.0%	100.0%	100.0%	$867.57*

Source: CRS calculations based on the 2009 IRS Statistics of Income (SOI) data, Table 3.3
http://www.irs.gov/taxstats/indtaxstats/article/0,,id=96981,00.html.

Notes: Items may not sum to 100% due to rounding. *-this figure reflects the average credit amount among all taxpayers.

The non-refundability feature of the Section 25C and Section 25D tax credits may limit who can claim these tax benefits. By definition, the value of a nonrefundable credit cannot exceed a taxpayer's tax liability. Although the Section 25D tax credit can be carried forward to offset tax liability in future years, the Section 25C credit can not be carried forward. Thus, taxpayers without sufficient tax liability in the current year can not benefit from the Section 25C credit. Taxpayers that eliminate their tax liability through claims of other tax incentives, such as those for the working poor, child-related tax incentives, and education tax benefits, are not able to benefit from certain tax-related residential energy-efficiency incentives.

**Figure 3. Distribution of the Residential Energy Tax Credits
by Claimants and Credit Amount, 2009**

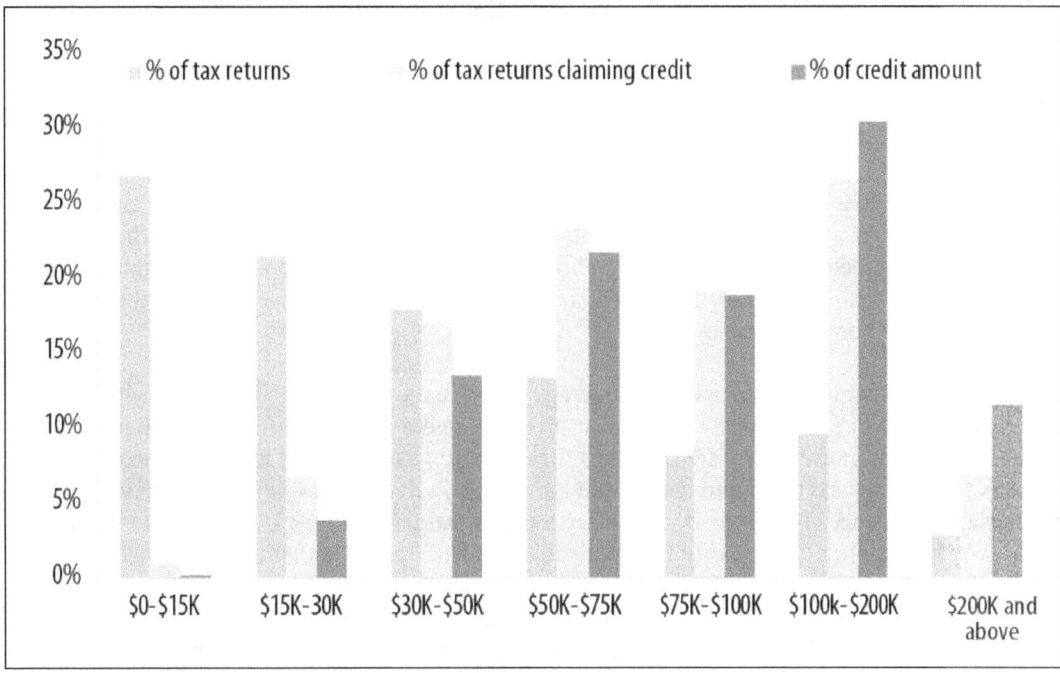

Source: CRS calculations based on the 2009 IRS Statistics of Income (SOI) data, Table 3.3
http://www.irs.gov/taxstats/indtaxstats/article/0,,id=96981,00.html.

Residential energy-efficiency tax incentives tend to be limited to higher-income taxpayers which may undermine one of the policy rationales behind using tax credits to motivate energy-efficiency investments. If households are not investing in energy-efficiency property because of the high up-front costs, and because these households are credit constrained, then tax credits that reduce this cost might encourage additional investment. However, if the tax credits are available only to higher-income households, households that are less likely to be credit constrained, then tax incentives may not be the most effective policy option for addressing this market barrier.

Administration: Are Energy-Efficiency Tax Credits Administratively Simple and Transparent?

An ideal tax code would be simple for taxpayers to comply with while also being simple for the government to administer. Taxpayers are more likely to claim tax benefits where compliance costs are low. If filing for certain tax benefits becomes too burdensome, eligible taxpayers might elect not to claim certain tax benefits, and therefore not respond to certain incentives delivered through the tax code.

There may be a trade-off, however, between allowing for tax credits with little reporting requirements and overall taxpayer compliance. In April 2011, the Treasury Department's Inspector General for Tax Administration (TIGTA) released a report on the residential energy tax credits which found that the processing of these credits provided numerous opportunities for fraud.[21] Specifically, TIGTA found that the IRS cannot verify whether individuals that claim either the Section 25C or Section 25D residential credit actually made qualifying energy modifications to their homes and whether the modifications they made were for their residence.

The IRS is unable to confirm that claimants of these credits are eligible for them when income tax returns are processed because they do not require taxpayers to provide information about the residences where they are installed, nor do they require third-party verification (i.e., receipts) that qualifying expenses were incurred. The form that taxpayers use to claim both of these credits, IRS Form 5695, does not ask taxpayers for any information that would confirm their eligibility for these credits. As a result, TIGTA was unable to confirm that 30% of taxpayers in their sample[22] who claimed the credits were even homeowners. The TIGTA report also noted that analysis of 2009 tax returns indicated that 5% of tax returns claiming these credits did not show any indication of homeownership.

TIGTA also found that 362 prisoners or underage individuals were allowed to claim $404,578 worth of these credits erroneously. Generally, prisoners and underage children will be ineligible for these credits because if they are prisoners for an entire year, they will tend to be unable to purchase the energy-saving improvements and underage individuals are unlikely to have purchased a residence. TIGTA made several recommendations to the IRS, including (1) revise Form 5695 to require the address of the applicable residence and whether that residence was a principal or secondary residence and (2) use available data on prisoners and underage individuals to ensure they are eligible for the residential energy tax credits. Notably, TIGTA did not recommend that the IRS also require third-party validation of qualifying expenditures. Although this information could be valuable in determining eligibility for these credits, it might also increase processing times and costs which would increase complexity for taxpayers and the IRS.

Policy Options[23]

The Section 25C and Section 25D tax credits are temporary provisions, and one policy option available to Congress is to allow these tax credits to expire as scheduled. Absent congressional action, the Section 25C credit for nonbusiness energy property will not be available after 2011. The Section 25D program is not scheduled to expire until the end of 2016. There may be other policy options Congress might want to consider regarding future incentives for residential energy efficiency, including modifying the credits or replacing them with a grant program.

Allow Tax Credits to Expire as Scheduled

One option regarding these credits is to let them expire as scheduled. For taxpayers who base their purchasing decisions on the availability of credits, this may result in taxpayers choosing not

---

[21] Treasury Inspector General For Tax Administration, *Processes Were Not Established to Verify Eligibility for Residential Energy Credits*, Reference Number: 2011-41-038, April 19, 2011, http://www.treasury.gov/tigta/auditreports/2011reports/201141038fr.pdf.

[22] TIGTA examined a statistically representative sample of 150 tax returns.

[23] The policy options discussed here include incentive-oriented options. Alternative policy options could be to impose regulations or standards mandating certain levels of energy efficiency. While standards and mandates may work to increase energy efficiency in newly installed property, imposing standards and mandates provide limited incentives for increasing efficiency in existing residential property.

to make eligible purchases after their expiration.[24] However, in so far as the credits are claimed by people who would make qualifying purchases absent these incentives, the expiration of these provisions would eliminate a windfall tax benefit while reducing revenue losses. Under current law, the Section 25D tax credit results in an estimated $0.2 billion in revenue loss annually. The one-year extension of the Section 25C tax credits enacted at the end of 2010 was estimated to result in $0.6 billion in revenue loss between 2011 and 2012.

Extend or Modify Current Tax Incentives

Policymakers may choose to extend, expand, or otherwise modify residential energy-efficiency tax incentives. As detailed in the legislative history in **Appendix B**, the current tax credits for residential energy efficiency have undergone a number of changes since being added to the code in 2005. Extending the credit in its current form, with the $500-per-taxpayer cap in place, would provide limited incentives for additional investment for homeowners that have already claimed tax credits under Section 25C. S. 3521, the Family and Business Tax Cut Certainty Act of 2012, would extend the 25C credit for two years—2012 and 2013. Extending the Section 25C tax credit through 2013 would cost an estimated $2.4 billion over the 2013 to 2022 budget window.[25]

These credits can be expanded in a variety of ways, including by calculating the credit using a more generous formula, expanding the types of technologies eligible for the credit, and by removing caps (both technology-specific and aggregate caps). Expansions may provide additional incentives that could encourage taxpayers to make more purchases. As illustrated in **Table B-1**, the value of these credits grew nearly five times between 2007 (when both Section 25C and Section 25D were in effect) and 2009 (when ARRA expanded these tax credits). Further, expansion of these credits may also provide additional windfalls to taxpayers who were going to make these purchases anyway.

Policymakers could also scale back these provisions in a variety of ways, including by reinstating technology-specific caps for the Section 25D credit, introducing an overall cap for the Section 25D credit (currently uncapped), reducing the technology-specific caps of Section 25C, or reducing the overall cap on Section 25C. Given that these would be changes from current policy, they may increase confusion among taxpayers when trying to estimate the size of their credits. Policymakers could also phase-out these credits for upper-income taxpayers who would be more likely to make eligible purchases without the credits. Extension of current policy, whether in current form, expanded, or scaled back, will have a greater budgetary cost than expiration of these benefits.

Replace Tax Credits with Grants or Rebates

Finally, policymakers may seek to replace these tax credits with a rebate program, or some alternative mechanism to provide direct cash payments to consumers for eligible purchases. This

---

[24] Alternatively, before the expiration of these provisions, taxpayers may increase their purchases of energy-efficient or renewable-energy-generating technologies to take advantage of these provisions before they expire.

[25] U.S. Congress, Joint Committee on Taxation, *Estimated Revenue Effects of the Revenue Provisions Contained in the "Family and Business Tax Cut Certainty Act of 2012," as Reported by the Senate Committee on Finance*, committee print, 112th Cong., 2nd sess., August 28, 2012, http://www.finance.senate.gov/legislation/details/?id=1cb48bce-5056-a032-5255-272274d52b64.

may be a more beneficial way to provide incentives to consumers purchasing energy-efficiency or renewable-energy-generating technologies, especially for consumers who do not have sufficient funds to make eligible expenditures and cannot wait until they file their taxes to receive a financial benefit from their purchases. Such a program could also benefit those with little or no tax liability who cannot benefit from nonrefundable tax credits. In 2010, both the House and Senate introduced legislation intended to create a rebate program, with rebates payable to contractors installing qualified energy-efficiency property.

The Home Star Energy Retrofit Act of 2010 (H.R. 5019 and S. 3177 and included in S. 3663) would have created a temporary two-tiered rebate program called Home Star. Its Silver Star program tier would have provided up to $3,000 per home in rebates for straightforward home upgrades, including insulation; efficient heating, ventilation, and air conditioning units; new windows; and other measures. The Gold Star program tier would have offered $3,000 rebates for more comprehensive energy retrofits achieving at least 20% energy savings, with rebates increasing up to $8,000 per home for retrofits achieving 45% energy savings.[26] Although some experts believed the Home Star program would result in an increased purchases of energy-efficiency improvements to homes, there were concerns that it could be more costly than expected (the legislation authorized $6 billion in appropriations), that there might be difficulties with its administration, and that it would not provide sufficient benefit to do-it-yourself repairs or improvements.[27] The legislation, which passed the House in 2010, was not considered by the Senate in the 111th Congress.

---

[26] For more information, see http://homestarcoalition.org/HOME_STAR_Overview.pdf.

[27] For more information on the Home Star program, including operational issues, see CRS Report R41273, *The Home Star Energy Retrofit Act of 2010: Operational and Market Considerations*, by Paul W. Parfomak.

Appendix A. Specifications for Property Eligible for Residential Energy-Efficiency Tax Credits

This appendix provides additional details on the technical standards for property to qualify for the tax credits in IRC Section 25C and Section 25D.

Table A-1. Nonbusiness Energy Property Tax Credit (§25C)

2011

Property	Qualifying Standard
Energy-efficiency Improvements to Building Envelope	
Insulation materials or systems	Meets 2009 International Energy Conservation Code (IECC) and Amendments
Windows, doors, and skylights	Must be Energy Star Qualified
Roofs	Metal roofs with appropriate pigmented coatings and asphalt roofs with appropriate cooling granules that also meet Energy Star requirements
Energy Efficient Property	
Electric Heat Pump (air source)	For split systems: Heat Seasonal Performance Factor (HSPF) ≥ 8.5, Energy Efficiency Ratio (EER) ≥ 12.5, Seasonal Energy Efficiency Ratio (SEER) ≥ 15. For package systems: HSPF ≥ 8, EER≥12, SEER ≥ 14
Central Air Conditioner	For split systems: SEER ≥ 16, EER ≥ 13. For package systems: SEER ≥ 14 and EER ≥ 12.
Natural Gas, propane or oil water heater	Energy Factor ≥ 0.82 or a thermal efficiency or at least 90%
Electric Heat Pump Water Heater	Energy Factor ≥ 2.0
Natural gas, propane, or oil furnace	Annual Fuel Utilization Efficiency (AFUE) ≥95
Natural gas, propane or oil water boiler	AFUE ≥ 95
Advanced main air circulating fan: $50	Must use no more than 2% of the furnace's total energy
Biomass Fuel Stoves	Thermal efficiency rating of at least 75%

Source: U.S. Department of Energy, Energy Star Program, http://www.energystar.gov/, *2011 Federal Tax Credits for Consumer Energy Efficiency* Updated November 16, 2010.

Notes: In 2011, the aggregate amount of credit is limited to $500. A taxpayer is ineligible for this tax credit if this credit has already been claimed by the taxpayer in an amount of $500 in any previous year, including 2009 and 2010 when the aggregate credit limits were higher. The credit is only available for expenditures for an existing home that is the taxpayer's principal residence. New construction and rentals do not qualify.

Table A-2. Residential Energy Efficient Property Tax Credit (§25D)

2011

Property	Qualifying Standard
Solar electric and solar water heating property	Qualifying property must be used exclusively for purposes other than heating swimming pools and hot tubs and must meet applicable fire and electrical code requirement. At least half of the energy generated by a solar water heating property must come from the sun and the system must be certified by the Solar Rating and Certification Corporation (SRCC) or a comparable entity endorsed by the government or the state in which the property is installed.
Fuel cell	Efficiency of at least 30% and must have a capacity of at least 0.5 kW
Small wind	Nameplate capacity of not more than 100 kW
Geothermal heat pumps	For closed loop: EER ≥ 14.1 and Coefficient of Performance (COP) ≥ 3.3. For open loop: EER ≥ 16.2 and COP ≥ 3.6. For direct expansion: EER ≥ 15 and COP ≥ 3.5

Source: U.S. Department of Energy, Energy Star Program, http://www.energystar.gov/, *2011 Federal Tax Credits for Consumer Energy Efficiency* Updated November 16, 2010.

Notes: Excluding fuel cell properties, the credit is available for expenditures for principal residences and second homes. Both existing homes and new construction qualifies. Rental units do not qualify. For fuel cell installations, the credit is restricted to principal residences (existing homes and new construction). Rentals and second homes do not qualify.

Appendix B. Legislative History

Tax credits for residential energy efficiency were first introduced in the late 1970s. These incentives were allowed to expire in the mid-1980s. The present-day residential energy tax incentives, introduced in 2005, are similar to the earlier incentives of the late 1970s and early 1980s.

Residential Energy Credits in the 1970s and 1980s

The Energy Tax Act of 1978 (P.L. 95-618) introduced the first tax credit for conservation and renewable-energy generation. Specifically this credit had two components. The first component was calculated as 15% of the first $2,000 of energy-conservation expenditures (a maximum credit value of $300). The second component was calculated as 30% of the first $2,000 in qualified expenditures for solar, wind, and geothermal energy plus 20% of the next $8,000 in qualified expenditures (a maximum credit value of $2,200). The final value of the credit was the sum of these two components, with the maximum value equaling $2,500. In 1980, Congress passed the Crude Oil Windfall Profit Tax Act of 1980 (P.L. 96-223), which increased the amount of the credit.[28] Specifically, this law increased the amount of the second component of the credit attributable to renewable energy generation to 40% of the first $10,000 of expenditures (yielding a maximum value of $4,000 for this component of the credit). This credit was allowed to expire at the end of 1985. Not until 2005, 20 years later, would Congress again enact federal tax credits for residential energy efficiency and renewable-energy property.

The Energy Policy Act of 2005

The Energy Policy Act of 2005 (EPACT05; P.L. 109-58) created two new temporary tax credits for homeowners who made energy-efficiency improvements to their homes. Under EPACT05, both credits were in effect for 2006 and 2007. The first credit was the nonbusiness energy property credit (IRC §25C). Under Section 25C, taxpayers were eligible for a nonrefundable tax credit equal to 10% of qualified expenditures, subject to certain limitations for specific types of property. Specifically, property-specific credit limits were $50 per year for any advanced main air circulating fan; $250 per year for any qualified natural gas, propane, or oil furnace or hot water boiler; and $300 for electric heat pumps, geothermal heat pumps, central air conditioners, and boilers and water heaters that met certain efficiency standards. The maximum amount of Section 25C credit that could be taken for windows over 2006 and 2007 was capped at $200. The lifetime cap for the Section 25C credit was $500 for 2006 and 2007.[29] The credit could only be applied to improvements made to the taxpayer's principal residence.

The second credit temporary established by EPACT05 for 2006 and 2007 was the residential energy-efficient property credit (IRC §25D). This nonrefundable credit was calculated as 30% of expenditures on qualified photovoltaic properties (where the sun's energy is used to generate

---

[28] For more information on the history of the credit in the late 1970s and early 1980s, see Robert McIntyre, "Lessons for Tax Reformers from the History of the Energy Tax Incentives in the Windfall Profit Tax Act of 1980," *The Boston College Law Review*, vol. 22, no. 705 (1981).

[29] In other words, if a taxpayer used $500 worth of §25C credit in 2006 for her home, she would be ineligible for the credit in 2007, irrespective of whether she had qualifying expenses in 2007.

electricity), solar water-heating properties (excluding those used for heating swimming pools and hot tubs), and fuel-cell generators, subject to annual limits. Specifically, the credit for photovoltaic and solar water-heating properties could not exceed $2,000 per year, whereas the credit for fuel cells could not exceed $500 per year. Qualifying photovoltaic and solar water-heating property expenditures included those made on any of the taxpayer's residences, whereas qualifying fuel-cell expenditures were limited to those made to the taxpayer's principal residence.

At the end of 2007, Section 25C expired. By contrast Section 25D was extended for the 2008 tax year by the Tax Relief and Health Care Act of 2006 (P.L. 109-432). Further, this act clarified that all property which used solar energy to generate electricity, not just photovoltaic property, could qualify for the Section 25D credit.

The Emergency Economic Stabilization Act (EESA)

In 2008, the Emergency Economic Stabilization Act of 2008 (EESA; P.L. 110-343) reinstated and modified the Section 25C credit for the 2009 tax year. EESA also expanded the list of qualified energy property to include biomass fuel stoves, which were eligible for a $300 credit. Geothermal heat pumps were removed from the list of eligible property under Section 25C but were added to the list of eligible property under Section 25D.

EESA extended the Section 25D tax credit for eight years, through 2016, modified it for existing technologies, and expanded it to new technologies. Specifically, the act eliminated the $2,000 maximum annual credit limit for qualified solar-electric property expenditures beginning in 2009. In addition, it expanded the credit to include expenditures for qualified small wind-energy property and (as previously mentioned) qualified geothermal heat pump property. The credit for qualified small wind energy was equal to 30% of expenditures made by taxpayers on a small wind-energy property up to a cap. The cap was set at $500 for each half kilowatt of electric capacity generated by a wind turbine, not to exceed $4,000 annually. The credit for qualifying geothermal heat pumps was calculated as 30% of expenditures up to a $2,000 annual cap for this technology. Taxpayers were eligible for the credits for both small wind-energy and geothermal properties installed on any of their residential properties.

The American Recovery and Reinvestment Act (ARRA)

The American Recovery and Reinvestment Act of 2009 (ARRA; P.L. 111-5) further extended and modified the Section 25C and Section 25D tax credits. With respect to the Section 25C credit, ARRA extended the credit for two years (2009 and 2010) and modified the calculation of the credit to be equal to 30% of qualified expenditures for energy-efficiency improvements and energy property, eliminating the technology-specific credit amounts.[30] In addition, the aggregate credit cap was lifted from $500 to $1,500 for 2009 and 2010 and the $200 aggregate cap for windows was eliminated for 2009 and 2010. Hence, if taxpayers used $1,000 of credit in 2009, their credit would be limited to $500 in 2010, irrespective if they had used this credit in 2006 and 2007. The removal of the aggregate cap for windows meant that in 2009 and 2010, taxpayers could claim up to $1,500 in tax credits for qualified windows. Finally, ARRA generally reduced

---

[30] The changes that ARRA made to the §25C credit in 2009 superseded the 2009 changes that had been made to the credit by EESA.

the efficiency standards for both energy-efficiency improvements and energy property, expanding the availability of the credit to additional products.

ARRA also changed the Section 25D tax credit for 2009 and 2010, primarily by removing the maximum credit caps for every type of technology except fuel cells. These changes were effective from 2009 through 2016.

Following the changes made to the Section 25C and Section 25D tax credits under ARRA, the number of credits being claimed and the total dollar amount of credits being claimed increased (see **Table B-1**). Further, under ARRA, average credit amounts were higher than they had been during 2006 and 2007, reflecting the higher credit rate.

Table B-1. Residential Energy Credits Claimed and Average Amount, 2006-2009

	Number of Tax Returns Which Include Claims for Residential Credits	**Total Amount of Residential Credits Claimed (Million)**	**Average Credit Amount**
2006	4,344,189	$1,000.15	$230
2007	4,326,398	$1,007.58	$233
2008	225,733	$216.69	$960
2009	6,711,682	$5,822.88	$868

Source: Internal Revenue Service, Statistics of Income (SOI), Individual Statistical Tables by Size of Adjusted Gross Income, Table 3.3, 2006-2009.
Notes: The Section 25C tax credit expired at the end of 2007 and was unavailable in 2008, hence the 2008 numbers represent claims for the Section 25D tax credit.

The 2010 Tax Act (P.L. 111-312)

Tax Relief, Unemployment Insurance Reauthorization, and Job Creation Act of 2010 (The 2010 Tax Act; P.L. 111-312) extended the Section 25C credit for one year, through the end of 2011. However, the credit structure returned to the structure that existed prior to the enactment of ARRA.[31] Importantly, the general lifetime limit ($500) and window lifetime limit ($200) were reinstated. Hence, if a taxpayer had claimed a total of $500 in Section 25C credits over 2006, 2007, 2009, and 2010 combined, they would be ineligible for the credit in 2011. Similarly if they had claimed $200 in credits for windows in 2006, 2007, 2009, and 2010 combined, they would be ineligible to claim the credit for windows in 2011. Additionally, certain efficiency standards that were relaxed under ARRA were restored to their prior levels. Finally, the technology-specific credit limits for energy-efficiency property were reinstated at pre-ARRA levels. Recently proposed legislation, S. 3521, the Family and Business Tax Cut Certainty Act of 2012, would extend the 25C credit for two years—2012 and 2013.

---

[31] The Section 25C credit in 2011 applies to asphalt roofs with cooling granules and biomass stoves, changes that were made by EESA.

Table B-2. Overview of Legislative Changes to the Nonbusiness Energy Property Tax Credit (§25C), 2005-2010

	2005	2008	2009	2010
	P.L. 109-58 (EPACT05)	P.L. 110-343 (EESA)	P.L. 111-5 (ARRA)	P.L. 111-312
Calculation of Credit	10% of Qualifying Energy-efficiency Improvements + Qualifying Energy Property (fixed by type. see below)	*	30% of Qualifying Energy-efficiency Improvements + 30% of Qualifying Energy Property (fixed amounts by property type eliminated)	10% of Qualifying Energy-efficiency Improvements + Qualifying Energy Property (capped by type)
Types of Qualifying Energy-efficiency Improvements to Building Envelope	(1) Insulation (2) Windows (Including skylights) (3) Doors (4) Qualifying Metal Roof	Added- (1) Asphalt Roof with cooling granules	*	*
Types of Qualifying Energy Property and Credit Amount	(1) Energy Efficient Building Property: $300 Electric Heat Pump (air source) Geothermal Heat Pump Central Air Conditioner Natural Gas, Oil or Propane Water heater Electric Heat Pump Water Heater (2) Natural gas, propane, or oil furnace: $150 (3) Natural gas, propane or oil water boiler: $150 (4) Advanced main air circulating fan: $50	Added- (1) Biomass fuel stoves: $300 Removed- (2) Geothermal heat pumps	Properties are unchanged, but fixed dollar amounts per property type are eliminated.	(1) Energy Efficient Building Property: $300 Electric Heat Pump (air source) Biomass fuel stoves: $300 Central Air Conditioner Natural Gas, Oil or Propane Water heater Electric Heat Pump Water Heater (2) Natural gas, propane, or oil furnace: $150 (3) Natural gas, propane or oil water boiler: $150 (4) Advanced main air circulating fan: $50
Aggregate Cap for Windows	$200 over all prior tax years	*	$200 aggregate cap for windows removed for 2009 and 2010	$200 (for all prior tax years beginning in 2006 including 2009 and 2010)
Aggregate Cap for Credit	$500 over all prior tax years	*	$1,500 over 2009 and 2010 (excludes expenditures in 2006, 2007)	$500 (for all prior tax years beginning in 2006 including 2009 and 2010)
Applicable Tax Years	2006 and 2007	2009	2009 and 2010	2011

Source: CRS analysis of P.L. 109-58, P.L. 110-343, P.L. 111-5, and P.L. 111-312.

Notes: * Unchanged from prior law.

Table B-3. Overview of Legislative Changes to Residential Energy-Efficient Property Tax Credit (§25D), 2005-2010

	2005 P.L. 109-58 (EPACT05)	2006 P.L. 109-432	2008 P.L. 110-343 (EESA)	2009 P.L. 111-5 (ARRA)
Calculation of Credit	30% of energy efficient property (subject to maximum credit amount by type of property, see below)	*	*	*
Qualifying Renewable Energy Generating Property and Max Credit Amount by Type of Property (includes labor costs)	(1) Solar electric (photovoltaic): $2,000 (2) Solar water heating: $2,000 (3) Fuel Cell: $500 per 0.5kW of power capacity	Clarified that all solar electric, not just photovoltaic property, qualified for the credit,	Added- (1) Small wind energy: $500 per 0.5kW power capacity up to $4,000 (2) Geothermal heat pumps: $2,000 (applicable from 2008-2016) Modified- (1) Solar electric (photovoltaic): max credit amount eliminated	Modified- (1) Small wind energy: max credit value eliminated (2) Geothermal heat pumps: max credit value eliminated (3) Solar water heating: max credit value eliminated
Aggregate Cap for Credit	None	*	*	*
Applicable Tax Years	2006 and 2007	2008	2009-2016	2009-2016

Source: CRS analysis of P.L. 109-58, P.L. 109-432, P.L. 110-343, P.L. 111-5, and P.L. 111-312.

Notes: * Unchanged from prior law.

Appendix C. Budgetary Impact of Residential Energy Tax Incentives

Table C-1. Revenue Losses Associated with Residential Energy-Efficiency Tax Incentives

billions of dollars

Provision	2006	2007	2008	2009	2010	2011	2012	2013	2014	2015
Credit for Energy Efficiency Improvements to Existing Homes (IRC §25C)	0.1	0.3	0.8	0.3	1.7	1.5	1.3			
Residential Energy Efficient Property Credit (IRC §25D)	-i-	-i-	-i-	0.1	0.2	0.2	0.2	0.2	0.2	0.2
New Energy Efficient Home Credit (IRC §45L)	-i-	-i-	-i-	-i-	0.1	-i-	-i-	-i-	-i-	-i-
Credit for the Production of Energy Efficient Appliances (IRC §45M)	0.1	0.1	0.1	0.1	0.2	0.2	0.1	-i-	-i-	-i-
Exclusion of Energy Conservation Subsidies Provided by Public Utilities (IRC §136)	-i-	-i-	-i-	-i-	-i-	-i-	-i-	-i-	-i-	-i-

Source: Joint Committee on Taxation.

Notes: An "-i-" indicates an estimated revenue loss of less than $50 million.

Author Contact Information

Margot L. Crandall-Hollick
Analyst in Public Finance
mcrandallhollick@crs.loc.gov, 7-7582

Molly F. Sherlock
Specialist in Public Finance
msherlock@crs.loc.gov, 7-7797